ARMY LEADERS
OF
WORLD WAR II

JAMES B. SWEENEY

Lieutenant Colonel,
U.S. Air Force (Retired)

Army Leaders OF World War II

Franklin Watts
New York | London | Toronto | Sydney | 1984
A First Book

Photographs courtesy of:
Bettmann Archive, Inc.: pp. 7, 14;
Fort Sam Houston, U.S. Army: p. 18;
Dwight D. Eisenhower Library: p. 23;
U.S. Army: pp. 26, 32, 69, 74;
Texas Military Institute: p. 37; UPI: pp. 40, 44;
Brooks Air Force Base, U.S. Air Force: p. 52;
U.S. Air Force Museum: pp. 53, 57; U.S. Air Force: p. 60;
Patton Museum of Cavalry and Armor: p. 64.

Library of Congress Cataloging in Publication Data

Sweeney, James B.
Army leaders of World War II.

(A First book)
Includes index.
Summary: Brief biographies of five outstanding
military leaders of World War II: George C. Marshall,
Dwight D. Eisenhower, Douglas MacArthur, Henry H. Arnold,
and George S. Patton, Jr.
1. World War, 1939–1945—Biography—Juvenile literature.
2. Generals—United States—Biography—Juvenile literature.
3. United States. Army—Biography—Juvenile literature.
[1. World War, 1939–1945—Biography.   2. Generals.
3. United States.   Army—Biography]   I. Title.
D736.S94 1984   940.53′092′2   [B]   [920]   84-7388
ISBN 0-531-04820-9

CONTENTS

This book is respectfully
dedicated to Howard
and Oma Lee Holland

INTRODUCTION

The deeds of the leader shall live,
and the hard-won glory of his exploits.

OVID

In the closing days of 1941, with the Japanese attack on Pearl Harbor, the United States was drawn into a global war. Ill-equipped and unready, the nation pressed forward to mobilize its defenses. It was during this dark period that Americans were to witness the emergence of military leadership of superior quality—leaders who were to make invaluable contributions to winning the war.

This is the story of five of those leaders: George C. Marshall, Dwight D. Eisenhower, Douglas MacArthur, Henry H. (Hap) Arnold, and George S. Patton, Jr.

Who were these men? Their personalities were different, their religious beliefs unalike, and their family backgrounds dissimilar. What then was the common thread that ran through their lives, that set them apart, that caused history to seize upon them and elevate them to greatness?

Too often, outstanding military leaders are seen as figures riding the crest of a wave. We envy them the honors, the accolades, but are rarely conscious of the years of study, service, and determination that preceded success. Victory is often attributed to luck—they were in the right place at the right time. This may be true, but it is also true that they were the right persons for the task. Luck? Yes, these leaders had luck, much of it good, but a modicum of it bad. So they took the good with the bad and warped it all into overwhelming success. They persisted, they believed in themselves, and when they spoke, it was with determination; when they acted, it was in a forthright way.

In the following pages, you will meet these five great army leaders—as they were in childhood, as they entered into military life, and as they made their marks in the annals of history.

ARMY LEADERS
OF
WORLD WAR II

Place of birth: Uniontown, Pennsylvania.

Date of birth: December 31, 1880.

Date of death: October 16, 1959.

Education: Virginia Military Institute, class of 1901.

Married: First marriage to Elizabeth Carter Coles, February 11, 1902. Second marriage to Katherine Tupper Brown, October 16, 1930.

Characteristics: Studious, given to details, somber, loyal, possessor of great leadership, diplomatic, soldierly in bearing, capable planner.

Major commands and accomplishments:
1919-24 staff officer to General John Pershing.
1924-27 China.
1936-37 commanded maneuvers.
1939-45 chief of staff.
1945   appointed ambassador to China.
1947   secretary of state.
1950   secretary of defense.
1953   received Nobel Peace Prize for his Marshall Plan.

GEORGE C. MARSHALL

The boy was proud of his discovery. He was related to Blackbeard the pirate. Best of all, he could prove this for a fact. It was printed in a book entitled *The Marshall Family*, that clearly stated that a young woman named Marshall had married the infamous pirate.

This was a matter of importance. Every youngster in the small village of Uniontown, Pennsylvania, knew of the doings of that venturesome sea rover. So little George Marshall had no difficulty in spreading the word. Some few intimates even got a glimpse of the book. The Marshall boy really strutted; he was Mister Somebody. Unfortunately, it wasn't long before the entire population of Uniontown knew of the Marshall family background. Word was out that the Marshalls came from a long line of pirates.

This was good for the boy, but bad for the father, who was a local businessman. George senior lowered the boom on George junior. He was thundering mad. "Let me tell you," he said in anger, "this book is only a half-true volume, poorly put together, by a distant relative named W. W. Paxton."

That deflated the boy's balloon. He was again just another student in a coal-mining town. Worse yet, neither he nor the village showed much promise. George C. Marshall, Jr., was born in Uniontown, Pennsylvania, on December 3, 1880. He had one living brother named William, and an older sister Marie. There had been another brother born before George, but he died at six months of age. His mother, Laura Bradford, of Augusta, Kentucky, and his father, George Catlett Marshall, were married on April 30, 1876.

As a student, young Marshall didn't quite measure up to the mark. He was a shy lad and, as often as possible, sidestepped recitations in which his shortcomings became obvious. Later, as was to be noted by biographers, George Marshall had indeed gotten off to a poor academic start. To compound a growing dislike for school, an elderly aunt named Eliza Stuart came to live with the Marshall family. She took it upon herself to improve the boy's studies. To accomplish this, she held teaching sessions on Saturday, a time when other neighborhood boys were to be heard outside playing baseball. In later years, the general himself admitted that Aunt Eliza Stuart "so soured me on study and teaching that I liked never to have recovered from it."

Schoolroom studies, which he disliked as a boy, were administered to him by attendance at Miss Alcinda Thompson's school in Uniontown. With indifference and practically no interest, he drifted through various grades until age ten. At that time, he was transferred to a public school. It was there, with quite a shock, he found himself poorly prepared to keep up with other students. His outlook for a bright future was not encouraging. Things seemed to be working against him. Not only was he shy, but he was somewhat tall and gangly, with sandy hair parted in the middle and a button-like nose. He was what teachers and students adjudged to be an unusually solemn person.

George C. Marshall
at the age of three

The one saving factor in young George's life was that his father happened to be an excellent reader. In those days, before radio or television, the written word held sway. In most families, it was the custom to gather in the evening while one member read from a book. With the Marshall family, it was acknowledged that the senior Mr. Marshall was a good reader. His selections were wise. Imaginative books, such as *The Deerslayer*, by James Fenimore Cooper (in which the Delaware Indians and a character named Natty Bumppo created an interesting yarn), and books by Conan Doyle (about a detective named Sherlock Holmes), plus many others, were all read aloud. It was great family entertainment and mentally stimulating. Gradually, the younger George Marshall found himself becoming interested in history—especially military history.

There were some advantages in growing up in a mountain village. Hunting and fishing were two of these. There was that river with the long Indian name—the Youghiogheny—which was full of trout and carp. Then there were those mountains with their endless supply of deer and small game. George Senior, an unbending type, would take the boy on bird hunting trips and, at times like those, relax to the point where he became a notch closer to his youngest son. Nevertheless, these were rare occasions. So young George found himself in a world without human warmth. His brother, six years older, was distant to him; while his sister, four years older, regarded him as somewhat of a pest. At school, he was neither liked nor disliked. Only through his mother did he attain some degree of worldly understanding.

Regardless, like any other growing boy, he managed to get into mischief. Somehow, he took to raising fighting cocks. That in itself was not illegal. But entering them into fights was against the law. George, too young to be seen near such clandestine meetings, had an older friend enter the birds in matches. In time, the local sheriff heard of the cockfights and tracked them down. Unexpectedly, he raided the secret cockpit where miners and farmers brought their roosters to fight. The sheriff and his deputies hit at the height of a meet, but George, hidden behind some trees, scampered off through the woods and was not caught. This close call was too vivid a warning. George abandoned the idea of raising fighting birds.

There were other minor happenings. He squirted his sister with a hose, did a bit of mischief with a BB gun and persistently annoyed his sister's boyfriends. "It was a wonder," she said later, "that I ever managed to get married."

However, it was his studies that gave his mother cause for worry. George was indifferent to learning. If he liked a subject, he excelled in it. But these were few. So his parents, in hopes of seeing him fired up, removed him from public school and sent him to a private academy for the last two years of high school. This new institution was called the University School. It was under the discipline of a man referred to as Professor Albert H. Hopkins. With this gentleman's push and shove, George Marshall managed to graduate from high school.

Sometime within these years of growing up, George was touched by a liking for the military. Perhaps it was his proximity to the Civil War, its battlefields and its veterans that triggered a desire to become a soldier. Even he, in later years, admitted that he could not say what, or when, the determination first crossed his mind. As poor luck would have it, attending West Point was out of the question. Both of Pennsylvania's elected senators were Republicans, as was Uniontown's single representative. George's father was a staunch and widely known Democrat. The chances of any one of these three Republican politicians nominating the son of a Democrat were so small, George never applied for admission to West Point. Nor is there any record that he did so at a later date. Instead, in 1897, he left Uniontown to enter Virginia Military Institute (VMI) as freshman, or, as they are called, a "rat."

It is difficult to say why George Marshall selected this Southern college. Perhaps those war stories told by a distant cousin,

Colonel Charles Marshall, who had been General Lee's aide, were of influence in the matter. At that time, the school, while it had high academic standards, and was strictly military, offered no assurances of being awarded a commission in the U.S. Army. For a sixteen-year-old Yankee, to enter a confederate college, so close to many bitter memories of the Civil War, is hard to explain. In later years, Marshall did admit to undergoing a good deal of hazing because of his Pennsylvania "twang." It was tough going, but at no time—even in later years—did Marshall complain about the rigorous life, the monotonous food, or tough studies.

Cadet George Marshall was not an especially brilliant student. His marks were always somewhere in the middle of the class. However, in military subjects and leadership, he was outstanding. In 1898, he led his class as first corporal, a high honor indeed. At the approach of his third year, his studies improved; he stood nineteenth in a class of forty-seven. In his final year, Marshall attained the highest honor in leadership, for he was named first captain.

Fortunately, his graduation in 1901 occurred at an advantageous time. The army, after years of neglect on the part of Congress, suddenly gained attention. The Philippine Islands had been under American control since 1899, ceded to the United States by Spain after the Spanish-American War. Abruptly, a Filipino leader named Emilio Aguinaldo led an insurrection against the United States. To meet this uprising, in 1901 Congress authorized an additional 35,000 U.S. Army volunteers. The force succeeded in capturing Aguinaldo and the revolt subsided into a series of guerilla skirmishes.

But the wheels of fate grind slowly. It was not until January 4, 1902 that Marshall received orders both appointing him a second lieutenant and assigning him to the Thirtieth Infantry with duty in the Philippines. But there were important matters yet to be concluded. During his student years he had fallen in love with a young woman named Elizabeth Carter Coles, called Lily. On the evening of February 11, 1902, they were married in her mother's house at Lexington, Virginia.

On April 12, 1902, Lieutenant Marshall boarded the troop transport for Manila. In July of that same year, President Theodore Roosevelt proclaimed peace. Marshall, now a member of Company G, Thirtieth Infantry, was stationed on the island of Mindoro. This was a steaming patch of mountainous jungle 4,000 square miles in size. Duty there was bug-ridden and torturous, plus the natives disliked Americans. Nevertheless, Marshall proved himself to be a good leader and a stern disciplinarian.

Luckily for Company G of the Thirtieth, they were relieved by elements of the Seventh Infantry in early November of that same year. They were then shipped to California aboard an army transport. Upon arrival, Company G was assigned to Fort Reno, in Oklahoma Territory. It was not until 1907 that the Oklahoma Territory was admitted as the forty-sixth state. However, in 1902, there were four companies of the Twenty-fourth Infantry; two companies of the Thirtieth Infantry; and one troop of the Eighth Cavalry. This was Indian country and to George Marshall an area he found to be most interesting. On the far side of a broad river marking the outer perimeter of the sturdy fort, was a reservation of the Arapahoe Indians. Soldiers were permitted to fish the river and hunt the land. Consequently, the military never lacked for things to do.

While life as a second lieutenant was interesting, and at times exciting, the pay was poor. Out of a monthly salary amounting to $116.67, he had to pay for uniforms, food and personal equipment, such as resolver, saber, field glasses, bed roll, mess kit and civilian clothes. Should an officer be married, he had to pay for shipping of family and their household goods.

Career officers frequently sought to better themselves by attending military specialty schools. Marshall applied for and was accepted to complete a one-year course at the Infantry and Cavalry School, Fort Leavenworth, Kansas. That was in the spring of

1906. Not only did he do well, he remained at the institution for four years, two of which as an instructor. These proved to be years in which he came to be seen and heard by numerous up-and-coming officers.

At about this time, trouble was brewing along the Mexican border. In 1911 it was decided to hold maneuvers in Texas. Troops were assembled in and about the city of San Antonio as a show of force. Marshall arrived in that area and was assigned to Company D of the Army Signal Corps. The maneuvers quickly brought to light the fact that this nation's National Guard was poorly trained and badly equipped. To remedy these deficiencies, a number of regular army officers were assigned as both inspectors and instructors for the National Guard. Lieutenant George Marshall was one of these men.

So he left San Antonio in May and undertook the giant task of moving from city to city in eastern Massachusetts. It is recorded that in one three-month period Marshall inspected forty-two companies in twenty-five cities and towns. Travel of this nature was not conducive to a good home life, but it was excellent for furthering a military career. As an outgrowth of such energetic devotion to duty, he was detailed to Governors Island in 1912. His task was to help plan a two-state exercise involving 15,000 men in National Guard units from New Jersey, New York, Connecticut, Massachusetts, Vermont, and Maine. These units were to be opposed by 2,300 regular army troops.

Following maneuvers and a series of new assignments, he was again ordered to the Philippines. In May of 1913, he reported to the Thirteenth Infantry in Manila. To Lieutenant George Marshall, this return to garrison duty lacked excitement and challenge. He started to find the army boring. In October 1915, he wrote to a friend that, "stagnation in promotion within the infantry has caused me to make tentative plans for resignation as soon as business conditions improve."

Luckily for America, conditions in the business world did not improve to such an extent that George C. Marshall submitted his resignation. For a war was brewing in Europe. A year before, Archduke Ferdinand of Austria was assassinated by a Serbian nationalist. Now charges and countercharges resulted in military combat. Germany, France, Great Britain, Russia, and Austria-Hungary were either involved or becoming so. The United States was not as yet entangled.

On May 1916, Marshall left the Philippines for Fort McDowell, San Francisco, California, to appear before a promotion board. Such was his excellent reputation that he was promoted to captain before ever reaching the board. This was fourteen years after he had first entered the army. During those days, that was a normal waiting period. Following this, he was assigned to training civilian volunteers, ages eighteen to fifty-three. He was so successful in this new undertaking that a superior officer, in writing a rating on Captain Marshall, stated that he would not only like to have Marshall under his command, but "I would prefer to serve *under his command.*" To this the colonel added that he thought Marshall to be a military genius and should be promoted to brigadier general.

In 1917, Germany declared its intention to wage unrestricted submarine warfare. Brutal action of such a nature struck at United States merchant shipping. This was a blow that the American people could not tolerate. President Wilson broke off diplomatic relations with Germany and Congress declared war on April 6, 1917.

The U.S. First Division, commanded by Major General W. L. Sibert, was the initial army unit to leave Hoboken, New Jersey, for Europe. Marshall was aboard the troop transport as a staff officer to Sibert. Things began to happen fast for the young captain. In December of 1917, an old friend, Major General Robert L. Bullard, took command of the division. In January of 1918, Marshall was moved into the most important position on the division's staff, that of Operations Officer, called G3.

Marshall as a member of General Bullard's staff in France during World War I

It is rare that a military staff officer receives recognition. Most often it is the field officer—the leader in combat—who is acclaimed. Marshall was the exception. He helped plan the American First Army's successful drive at Saint-Mihiel, in France. Following that, Marshall, by now a colonel, was assigned a massive task. General John J. Pershing, then in charge of American troops overseas, ordered him to plan the secret movement of forces from Saint-Mihiel to the French Meuse-Argonne front. This meant the quick shifting of 500,000 soldiers, 2,700 heavy guns, and thousands of tons of combat material from one battle zone to another. Marshall, in order to maintain the necessary secrecy, made the transfer at night. He accomplished the almost impossible task within a two-week period.

General Pershing, now fully aware of Marshall's potential, submitted his name for promotion to brigadier general. Due in part to Marshall's own successful efforts, World War I ended before Congress could approve the promotion. Shortly after the war, Pershing was made chief of staff. Wisely, he took Marshall along as his aide. After six years in that influential position, Marshall was assigned to the Fifteenth Infantry at Tientsin, China. This was in July of 1924. Following his tour of duty, he was appointed to be an instructor at the Army War College. Shortly after moving to Washington, D.C., his wife became seriously ill and died on September 15, 1927.

The Infantry School at Fort Benning, Georgia, was then Marshall's next assignment. He was named assistant commandant and placed in charge of the academic department. His tour of duty at the school, from 1927 to 1932, was during some of the worst days of the depression. Married enlisted soldiers under his command, earning from twenty-one dollars a month to slightly more, found it impossible to feed and clothe their families on such meager pay. To alleviate any suffering, Marshall established a system whereby an enlisted soldier could buy sufficient hot food from the company mess for mere pennies. This insured wife and children receiving at least one hot meal a day. During this time, on October 16, 1930, Marshall remarried. His second wife was a widow, Katherine Tupper Brown.

The depression was changing things. Marshall was assigned as a battalion commander to Fort Screven, Georgia. This post was then designated district headquarters for the newly created Civilian Conservation Corps (CCC), in an area composed of South Carolina, eastern Georgia, and Florida. After this difficult tour, he was designated senior army instructor for the Illinois National Guard. In 1936, Marshall was promoted to brigadier general and placed in command of the Fifth Infantry Brigade, part of the Third Division, and stationed at Vancouver Barracks in the state of Washington.

On February 27, 1938, Marshall was transferred to Washington, D.C. There he served as deputy chief of staff, until President Roosevelt appointed him acting chief of staff on July 1, 1939. On September 1, 1939, Germany invaded Poland. World War II was under way. At that time he went from a one-star brigadier general to a full general with four stars and officially became chief of staff.

Prior to 1939, Marshall had been pushing for a reorganization and expansion of the army. Neglect had let its numbers dwindle to 174,000 persons and less than 1500 aircraft. With typical Marshall persuasiveness, he induced Congress into the enactment of a peacetime draft. Before his efforts were concluded, the U.S. Army had grown to nearly 9,000,000 persons and 75,000 planes in 1945. In addition to the management of this gigantic buildup, he foresaw America's involvement in the war and worked quietly with Great Britain in formulating plans for a firm partnership. On December 7, 1941, his insight into world trends was borne out when Japan attacked Pearl Harbor. Congress declared war on Japan. On December 11, Germany and Italy declared war on the United States.

Now began Marshall's greatest military and political struggle.

He designed a basic plan to win World War II: first, knock out Germany, then turn Allied attention to winning in the Pacific. His approach to victory was approved by President Roosevelt. However, it was opposed by other political forces. General Douglas MacArthur, the U.S. Navy, a number of Congressmen, and a segment of the public, all felt that Japan should be attacked first. Additionally, Winston Churchill, on behalf of British military leaders, requested that American forces first be thrown into combat in the Mediterranean theater. Marshall held firm to his plan— a lethal attack against Germany, via an invasion of France.

Great Britain had agreed that the country supplying the greatest number of troops would also supply the commander. Marshall wanted this job. However, President Roosevelt told him, "I didn't feel I could sleep at ease if you were out of Washington." It was therefore Dwight D. Eisenhower who received the enviable invasion command. Regardless, Marshall gave General Eisenhower his full backing throughout the war. In 1944, Marshall received his fifth star, thereby becoming a General of the Army.

With the conclusion of World War II, General Marshall's service to his country continued. In 1945, President Truman appointed him to head a mission to China. He ended his China mission in January 1947, on a successful note. On his return from China, he was appointed secretary of state. He was the only army officer ever to hold this high office. It was in June of that year, in a speech before the Harvard graduating class, he revealed a massive plan for world recovery. Basically, it was an arrangement whereby each European country decided on its own economic needs, toward which the United States would then lend assistance. The suggestion caught on and in April of 1948, President Truman signed the Economic Cooperation Administration (ECA) into law. This became known as the Marshall Plan. For his efforts in international recovery, Marshall received the Nobel Prize in 1953. General Marshall then brought his long career of public service to an end in 1951 after serving one year as secretary of defense.

Dean Acheson, the statesman who succeeded General Marshall as secretary of state, payed his predecessor a great tribute. He wrote, "There is no military glamour about him and nothing of the martinet. Yet to all of us he was always 'General Marshall.' The title fit him as though he'd been baptized with it."

General George C. Marshall died on October 16, 1959. He is buried at Arlington National Cemetery, Washington, D.C.

General of the Army
George C. Marshall

Place of birth: Denison, Texas.

Date of birth: October 14, 1890.

Date of death: March 28, 1969.

Education: West Point, class of 1915.

Married: Mamie Geneva Doud, July 1, 1916.

Nickname: Ike.

Characteristics: A born leader, likeable, tactful, strong temper (which he learned to control), diplomatic.

Major commands and accomplishments:

1926 graduated first in class, Command and General Staff School.

1933 assistant to chief of staff General Douglas MacArthur.

1941 chief of staff, Third Army.

1942 commanded invasion of North Africa.

1944 supreme commander, Allied Expeditionary Forces; directed invasion of Normandy.

1945 accepted surrender of Germany; became chief of staff, United States Army.

1948 named president of Columbia University.

1950 appointed supreme commander of NATO.

1952 elected president of the United States.

1961 retired from public life to home in Gettysburg, Pennsylvania.

1969 died on March 28, at Walter Reed Hospital, Washington, D.C.

DWIGHT D. EISENHOWER

One of the world's greatest generals learned his first lesson in military tactics at four years of age. The event took place on a family farm north of Topeka, Kansas. A male goose (called a *gander*), was looking after its flock when it spotted a small boy walking into its territory.

The youngster was curious about the strange looking bird. "Hmmm," he thought to himself as he came closer to the web-footed animal that resembled a swan. "Just a harmless duck of some sort."

Suddenly the peaceful-appearing bird spread a pair of broad wings, shot out a long neck, opened a frightening-looking beak and came hissing at the pint-sized intruder. To a four-year-old boy, who had never seen a gander before, the oncoming bird was a terrifying sight. The lad turned and ran for the house.

Indoors, a warm hug from Aunt Minnie—and a fresh-baked cookie to boot—stifled the boy's sobs. Nevertheless, the gander had won this initial showdown. A pattern was set. Whenever the combative bird spotted the hesitant child, it charged. The boy never failed to scamper indoors for one of Aunt Minnie's reassuring hugs.

Not so with Uncle Luther. He witnessed his nephew's daily confrontations and defeats. Something had to be done to reverse the trend. Taking an old broom, he clipped off most of the straw. He then presented this to Dwight with instructions on how it was to be used as a defensive weapon. "Now," he said, "I want you to go out and show that old bird who's boss of the barnyard."

The wavering lad stepped outdoors. Cautiously, he began to walk toward a not-too-distant barn. The gander saw its quarry coming. It ruffled its feathers and readied itself for the usual victory charge. With animal cunning, it let the youngster get midway between house and barn. This time there would be no escape for the human. The boy was in for a severe pecking. Suddenly, the bird burst into a flapping, hissing rush.

Then a horrible thing happened. The boy whooped out a battle cry and dashed to meet the oncoming gander. Abruptly, the field of combat reversed itself. The bird, unfamiliar with such tactics, turned to flee—only to receive a thump from the boy's broom. "And that," Dwight Eisenhower was to recall many years later, "taught me never to negotiate with an enemy except from a position of strength."

David Dwight Eisenhower (later he transposed his first and middle names to Dwight David) was born in Denison, Texas, to David and Ida Eisenhower. He was the third son in what later was to be a family of seven sons, one of whom died in infancy. Shortly after Dwight's birth, the family moved to Abilene, Kansas. It was a hard-working group, with roots that went back beyond the Civil War and on into Germany. They were a religious family, practicing daily reading of the Bible. The father, after whom Dwight David was named, took a job as plant engineer at the Belle Springs Creamery. In later years, with what little savings they had, the father built a house on a small tract of land. Like so many other western towns, Abilene was cut down the middle by railroad tracks. As luck would have it, the Eisenhower house was on what was considered "the wrong side of the tracks." Socially, as well as economically, the family was thought of as "blue collar."

*The young Dwight D. Eisenhower is
shown here on a camping trip with friends.
Ike is in the foreground.*

Regardless, as General Eisenhower was often heard to say, "If we were poor, we weren't aware of it."

But hard work was the lot of such folks. Each of the boys had an assigned number of chores to perform. Not all were enjoyable, such as the one Dwight found intensely distasteful. It came about in this manner. The small farm yielded a given amount of fresh vegetables. It was up to the boys to load these onto a wagon and huckster them to residents on the other side of the railroad tracks. The well-to-do housewives had a way of making the Eisenhower boys feel like beggars. They would strip the corn to see if it was fresh, thumb the melons to discover if they were ripe, and brazenly pop a sample strawberry into their mouths to taste its sweetness. Then, after such conduct, they'd haggle over the price. To Dwight, these actions were demeaning.

Dwight, like other boys of his age, went to high school. To do so, he had to work after classes at whatever job he could find. Ambitious, full of energy, and eager to progress, Dwight nevertheless found time for athletics. He was on both the school baseball and football teams. During his last year, he was elected president of the Abilene High School Athletic Association. The school yearbook, named the *Helianthus,* said that Dwight was their best historian and mathematician. It also predicted that he would become a professor of history at Yale University. Dwight D. Eisenhower graduated from high school in May of 1909. At that time he weighed 145 pounds (65.8 kg), was five feet eleven inches (1.8 m) tall, and possessed a solid frame. In addition he was said to have a strong will and an explosive temper.

There is always some one factor, or person, that motivates a youngster into applying for admission to West Point. In the case of Dwight Eisenhower, it was a friend named Swede Hazlett. Swede had his mind set on a military career and suggested that his friend Dwight also try the entrance exams for both West Point and Annapolis. Eisenhower did so and was amazed when informed that he'd scored the highest for Annapolis and second highest for West Point. At this juncture, luck intervened. The young man who scored first for West Point could not pass the physical exam. This left Dwight D. Eisenhower number one on the list. He therefore had the choice of going to either school. He went to West Point.

On June 2, 1911, Dwight Eisenhower took the train to New York and, ultimately, to four years at West Point. On June 12, 1915, he received his commission as a second lieutenant. He had placed sixty-first in a class of 164, which ranked him in the upper half of his class. At that time, he was almost twenty-five years of age. Because of a previously injured knee, there was some doubt that this newly commissioned officer would be assigned to active duty. In those days the regular army of the United States totaled only 120,000 men. There was little room for newly commissioned second lieutenants. However, after some uncertainties, Eisenhower was given orders to report to Fort Sam Houston, Texas. Unbeknownst to anyone of that era, the West Point class of 1915 was to become known as "The Class the Stars Fell On." Two World Wars produced an enormous need for general officers. This necessity touched upon the class of 1915. Out of 164 cadets, fifty-nine attained the rank of general. Of this group, both Eisenhower and Omar N. Bradley became five-star generals, while Joseph McNarney and James Van Fleet became four-star generals.

In 1916, Second Lieutenant Dwight Eisenhower married Mamie Geneva Doud, who had been born in Boone, Iowa. They had two sons, Doud Dwight and John Sheldon Doud. The first born, Doud Dwight, died of scarlet fever.

There was trouble brewing throughout the world, and it was not long before this country was drawn into World War I. Eisenhower, seeing development of a new implement for combat, transferred from the infantry to the tank corps. Although he was not sent overseas, he attained the rank of lieutenant colonel while in charge of Camp Colt, Pennsylvania, a tank training center. Following the war, all United States tank forces were assembled at Fort Mead, Maryland. It was there that he and George S. Patton, Jr., became acquainted and formed a lasting friendship. After an

Newlyweds Lieutenant and Mrs. Eisenhower

assignment in the Panama Canal Zone, Dwight Eisenhower was sent to the Command and General Staff School at Fort Leavenworth, Kansas, as a student. He graduated number one in the class of 1926. Two years later, in 1928, he graduated from the Army War College, at Carlisle, Pennsylvania, with distinction.

Assignments were rapid fire for the young officer. His potential was beginning to be recognized. He was sent to France as a member of the Battle Monuments Commission. Later, he played a part in establishing the Army Industrial College, after which he served with the army chief of staff's office under Douglas MacArthur. When General MacArthur left for the Philippines in 1935, he took Dwight Eisenhower with him as his aide.

In the fall of 1939, Eisenhower was assigned to Fort Lewis, Washington. There he was placed in charge of a battalion belonging to the Fifteenth Infantry Division. And it was there that he met with his friend Mark W. Clark, another West Point graduate, who was operations officer (G3) for the division. One year after reporting in at Fort Lewis, Eisenhower was assigned to be chief of staff of the Twenty-second Corps. Again, one year later, he became chief of staff for General Walter Krueger's Third Army.

At about this time, the Louisiana maneuvers were staged in preparation for possible involvement with Nazi Germany. Because of Dwight Eisenhower's brilliant work during these maneuvers, he was brought to the notice of General George C. Marshall, who was then U.S. Army chief of staff. Eisenhower was promoted to brigadier general.

The Japanese attack on Pearl Harbor occurred in December of 1941, and the newly promoted general was brought to Washington and placed in charge of the War Plans Division of the General Staff. Regardless of what was happening in the Pacific, there were certain commitments that had to be honored. The United States had previously promised Great Britain that, in the event of war, we would make an all-out effort to assist the English in their battle against Hitler. Any development in the Far East would be placed in a holding pattern until after a Nazi surrender was accomplished. As part of this European plan, troops, supplies and combat equipment were to be sent to England as soon as possible. This required a great deal of planning and some smart management. General Marshall was well aware of the enormity of the problem. He ordered Eisenhower to go to London and take charge of the American forces in Britain. His job would be to lay plans for an influx of well-equipped Americans and to work out future joint battlefield tactics. There should be no friction between the two forces. Everything had to run smoothly.

Eisenhower so impressed the British people with whom he worked—including the prime minister, Winston Churchill—that General Marshall appointed him commander of the "European Theatre of Operations," later to become known as ETO. In his turn, General Eisenhower placed General Mark Clark in command of the Second Corps. This was to be the headquarters officially reponsible for the combat training of all American units arriving in the United Kingdom.

Winston Churchill recommended to President Roosevelt that Anglo-American landings be made in the French-held portion of North Africa. Roosevelt agreed and, because of traditional French-American friendship, the American forces were the first ashore. It was hoped that those Vichy French forces under German domination would refuse to fire on their friends. To further this hope, General Eisenhower established an Allied headquarters to plan and direct the gigantic operation. The backbone of the design became an integrated staff. An American and a British officer filled each staff position. This was a new concept in the waging of war. It required that every officer work in harmony toward a unified goal. Because of Eisenhower's strong personality and tactfulness the system worked. Political plans were kept at the highest level. All major differences were settled by Winston Churchill and President Roosevelt. Eisenhower's job was to counsel, encourage, instruct, and oversee the team.

While Allied harmony was maintained reasonably well within

upper echelons, it broke down at lower staff levels. Although British officers joined American officers for coffee breaks, and vice versa for tea breaks, operational differences frequently turned into angry shouting matches. This infuriated Eisenhower. On two occasions he ordered American officers relieved of command and sent home. Once Eisenhower's determination to attain integrated accord became apparent, men strove to reconcile differences. Unfortunately, there were personality clashes at all levels. America's General George Patton disliked Britain's Field Marshal Bernard Montgomery, who reciprocated in equal measure. France's Charles De Gaulle felt slighted by Winston Churchill and vacillated between obeying commands or ignoring them. However, Eisenhower was a strong-willed man. He could handle such matters—and he did.

North Africa was not an easy victory. Fighting took place, but Eisenhower cleverly secured an armistice within three days. He did so by use of a controversial French officer named Admiral François Darlan. A great furor was created over the use of Darlan, as he, at one time, had collaborated with the Germans. Regardless of the uproar created in both England and America, Eisenhower held to his plan as a means of saving the lives of American fighting men. The clamor finally ended in an abrupt manner—a Frenchman assassinated Darlan.

Eisenhower had hopes of closing out the North African campaign by the end of 1942. However, the Nazi buildup of forces in Tunisia dragged the fighting into 1943. Because of numerous unforeseen problems, the Allied forces became weakened as a strike force. The Germans took advantage of these weaknesses. In February of 1943, they launched an all-out attack against Eisenhower's forces. Only a heroic stand by Allied troops at Sbiba and Kasserine passes prevented a breakthrough.

Eisenhower was aware of Allied weaknesses. To offset these shortcomings, he reorganized his forces. He placed a British general, Sir Harold Alexander, in charge of ground forces within North Africa. He then placed General George Patton in command of U.S. forces in Tunisia. By March of that year, Allied forces defeated the Axis and early in May captured Tunis, Bizerte and 250,000 enemy troops. Eisenhower's North Africa strategy had won.

It had previously been agreed that Sicily would be the next point of Allied attack. Even before the fall of North Africa, Eisenhower's strategy against Sicily had been mapped out. He ordered that Axis air bases on the islands of Pantelleria and Lampedusa be subjugated by naval gunfire. This order met with tremendous opposition from numerous members of the Allied officer staff. Many felt that an army landing would be required and should therefore be organized. Eisenhower stuck to his war plan. He proved to be right. Both islands surrendered and were quickly converted into Allied air bases.

These two air bases then afforded air cover for the Allied invasion of Sicily. On July 10, 1943, General George Patton and Sir Bernard Montgomery landed their forces. After thirty-eight days of fierce fighting, Sicily fell. On July 25, Benito Mussolini, the Italian dictator, was toppled from power. His replacement was Marshal Pietro Badoglio. Using General Maxwell Taylor as his emissary, General Eisenhower tried to attain a quick settlement of the Italian situation. Unfortunately, it was not to be, for Badoglio stalled on signing an agreement of complete surrender until September 3, 1943 (when a secret armistice was signed). The capitulation was announced publicly by all concerned on September 8. The Allies were then able to occupy Italy by crossing the Strait of Messina from Sicily.

Eisenhower's next move was programmed for the spring of 1944. It was called "Operation Overlord," and was the invasion of the Normandy area of France. This was to be the final thrust that would drive a wedge into the heart of Germany. A great deal of pre-invasion planning was needed. During January of 1944, Eisenhower secretly went to Washington, D.C. to confer with President Roosevelt, General Marshall, and numerous other government officials. He quickly completed these consultations and returned to London. There, he immediately established the Supreme Headquarters, Allied Expeditionary Force. This placed him in command of all Allied land, sea and air forces to be used in the cross-channel invasion of mainland Europe. In this capacity he insisted that three airborne divisions be dropped at Normandy before the landing of seaborne forces.

The date for the Normandy invasion was set for June 5. However, a vicious storm blew up and produced high winds and gigantic seas. Eisenhower ordered the operation postponed for one day. Upon checking with meteorologists, Eisenhower learned that on June 6, the weather would begin to improve. In what has since been termed one of the war's most courageous decisions, Eisenhower decided to attack, his reasoning being that the Germans would feel certain that it would be foolhardy for anyone to attack during such a storm. They understimated the determination and will power of Eisenhower. He attacked.

In doing so he caught the Axis forces by surprise. Although fierce fighting took place, Allied beachheads were established. Within a relatively few days, they formed a uniform line of attack. More men, weapons, and supplies were able to be brought in. The beachhead was united, strengthened, and better organized. Still, the going was never easy for Allied forces. The countryside was rough and suitable for the Germans to defend. Panzer commanders threw every tank available into a vain effort to drive the Allies into the sea. For a while it was touch and go. Then, in the latter part of June, Lieutenant General Omar Bradley, the American field commander, gained air superiority and launched operation COBRA. This was the code name for an Allied breakthrough at Normandy. As commander, Bradley employed infantry troops to slash an opening in enemy lines, thus allowing his armored forces to drive through the gap. Eisenhower, recognizing an opportunity, swung two of his American armies toward the east, thus encircling German forces. Having been successful in this, Eisenhower ordered his troops to thrust on. In short order they jumped the Seine River and moved toward Germany itself.

Eisenhower talks with paratroopers just before they board their airplanes to take part in the Normandy invasion.

As Allied forces entered Belgium on September 2, Eisenhower linked his loosely scattered invasion forces into a cohesive command. Unfortunately, because of rapid forward progress, American mechanized columns began to run short of supplies. Gasoline, food, and ammunition ran low. Severe winter weather added to difficulties and suffering. It was then that the Germans launched what was to become known as the "Battle of the Bulge." Nazi forces drove a wide salient into American lines. Fierce fighting ensued. Eisenhower wasted no time; he rushed reinforcements into the line of battle. By late January of 1945, the bulge in the Allied lines was straightened and no longer a threat.

By March 7, Allied forces were pouring across the Rhine River at numerous points. Because of political plans previously agreed upon by Roosevelt, Churchill, and Stalin, Eisenhower was forced to halt his troops and allow the Russians to occupy Berlin. As the war in Europe came to a close, it became evident that General Dwight Eisenhower had fulfilled his difficult assignment. Having been given a number of headstrong field commanders, who were both aggressive and competent, he nevertheless adhered to orders and instructions as issued by General Marshall. A man of great capabilities, he served as chief of American Occupation forces until November 1945, when he returned to the United States and was appointed chief of staff. Still later, he became president of Columbia University. Following that, he was appointed supreme commander of NATO forces in Europe. The North Atlantic Treaty Organization was signed into being on April 4, 1949 by the ministers of Belgium, Canada, Denmark, France, Great Britain, Iceland, Italy, Luxembourg, the Netherlands, Norway, Portugal, and the United States. Other nations, such as Greece, Turkey, and West Germany, joined at a later date. Following this, Eisenhower then went on to serve as president of the United States for two terms. On March 28, 1969, he died at Walter Reed Army Hospital, Washington, D.C., after suffering a heart attack. His body was transported to Abilene, Kansas, for final burial.

Place of birth: Arsenal Barracks, Little Rock, Arkansas.

Date of birth: January 26, 1880.

Date of death: April 5, 1964.

Education: West Point, class of 1903.

Married: Twice. First marriage to Louise Cromwell Brooks, February 14, 1922. Second marriage to Jean Fairchild, April 30, 1937.

Characteristics: Arrogant, noble, flamboyant, imperious, intellectual, shy, brave, charming, temperamental.

Major events, commands, and accomplishments:
1906 appointed aide to President Theodore Roosevelt.
1908 reprimanded twice for insubordination.
1914 recommended for Congressional Medal of Honor.
1917 assigned as chief of staff, Rainbow Division.
1919 became superintendent of West Point.
1920 promoted to brigadier general.
1930 named Army chief of staff.
1936 became Philippine field marshal.
1941 named Far East commander by President Franklin Roosevelt.
1942 escaped to Australia.
1945 Manila, Bataan, Corregidor retaken; Japanese surrendered to MacArthur aboard U.S.S. *Missouri*.
1946 became ruler of 83 million Japanese.
1950 became first United Nations commander; ordered to conquer North Korea.
1951 stripped of all commands by President Truman.
1952 entered political arena by giving keynote speech at Republican National Convention.
1964 begged President Johnson to stay out of Vietnam; died and was entombed in Norfolk, Virginia.

DOUGLAS MACARTHUR

The sound of military bugles was Douglas MacArthur's first memory of life. Even as a toddler, he lived by the notes of a trumpet. Reveille, and it was time to get up; mess call, and it was time to eat; retreat, and it was nearing bedtime. Unfortunately, not all bugle calls were so routine. Too often the bone-chilling notes of *to arms, to arms* would blast through the compound. Then it was boots and saddles and a column of horsemen jangling by at a canter.

Such was life in a frontier fort on January 26, 1880, when young Douglas MacArthur was brought squalling into the world, the third son born to Mary and Arthur MacArthur. For his father was captain of Company K, Thirteenth Infantry, and at that time was out in the wilds fighting Indians. Not just any Indians—Apache Indians being led by an able chief named Geronimo. But the birth did not go unnoticed. One newspaper reported this happening by announcing to its readers that a Douglas MacArthur had been born "while his parents were away."

By the time he was three years old, his father was stationed at Fort Wingate. There his oldest brother died. Following that, Company K of the Thirteenth was transferred to Fort Selden. This was a newly created post close by the Rio Grande. MacArthur remembered it, fondly, as a place of adobe buildings, intense heat, wooden palisades, outside privies, and candles for light. It was wildish country, full of game, and the coming and goings of such notorious characters as Buffalo Bill, Wild Bill Hickok and others who left their mark on frontier history. In a sense, it was a boy's paradise. MacArthur learned to hunt, ride horses, track game, handle weapons, and listen while his elders told war stories.

At thirteen, his father was transferred to Fort Sam Houston, just outside San Antonio, Texas. It was there his formal military education commenced. He was sent to the Texas Military Institute as a day student. Here he not only met formal book learning for the first time, but competition from others of his own age. He learned to enjoy both. When his fourth year came around, Douglas MacArthur was number one in his class.

Not all was easy going for the boy. He wanted to enter West Point, but West Point did not want him. He had curvature of the spine and therefore could not pass the physical test. However, neither the congressmen, who were needed to make an appointment, nor the U.S. Army had reckoned with Douglas MacArthur's mother. Known to her friends as "Pinky," she was an iron-willed woman who was ambitious for her son. Medical treatment took care of the fault in her son's back and politics took care of the appointment. Pinky played a tough game of hard ball. When Douglas MacArthur was finally permitted to take the competitive examination, his marks totaled 99.5; the nearest man's score was a mere 77.9. One year later, in 1899, both Douglas MacArthur and his mother took the train for West Point. Once there, young Douglas became a cadet, while Pinky took up residence nearby to become known as his mother-in-residence. She was to occupy this position until her death.

Douglas MacArthur as a cadet
at Texas Military Institute

[36]

CLASS OF 1897

No student ever said that West Point was easy. Douglas MacArthur was no exception. The going was hard. Life at the Point, during those days, was cloistered almost beyond belief. Students were allowed off the grounds on only two occasions: for the annual Army-Navy football game, and for a short summer vacation. It was just studies, drill, formations, and examinations. Hazing, or harassing by abusive and humiliating tricks, was a big part of the scene. Upperclassmen rode herd on new arrivals to a brutal extent. In fact, so severe did this way of life become, that one student died as a result of hazing. This brought on a Congressional investigation. Cadet MacArthur was called to testify, but managed to conduct himself in a noteworthy manner. His mother, of course, was nearby to lend moral support and advice.

June 11, 1903 saw Douglas MacArthur graduate first in his class from West Point, be commissioned a second lieutenant and assigned to the corps of engineers. On joining the engineers, he became aide to his father. After that, he went on to serve as aide to President Theodore Roosevelt (1906–07). During World War I he was named chief of staff of the Rainbow Division. This was an unofficial designation given the Forty-second Division. It was the first combat division to arrive in France. Once there, it fought in the second battle of the Marne. It was also used to spearhead attacks at Saint Mihiel and in the Meuse-Argonne sector. During these campaigns the division suffered heavy casualties.

Following months of bitter fighting, MacArthur became known as "the dude." This was because of his eccentric mode of dress, a long woolen muffler, crushed officer's cap, turtleneck sweater, loosely fitting field jacket, and swagger stick. Yet no man dared laugh at his peculiarity, for he was wounded several times, cited nine times for bravery and decorated upon various occasions. In June of 1920 he was promoted to brigadier general, thus becoming the youngest American division commander.

After World War I, MacArthur served as superintendent of West Point. This was from 1919 to 1922. During these years he made many changes. Regional entrance exams for the Point were made uniform and more stringent, the syllabus was modernized, updated military training was implemented, and disciplinary rules were modified. During 1925, MacArthur became the army's youngest major general when he received his second star. In October of 1930, he was named to be chief of staff of the U.S. Army.

These were horrible years for the American public. The stock market crash of 1929 had brought on a worldwide depression. But MacArthur was not idle during these times of low budgets, poor salaries, hunger, and mass unemployment. Congress slashed appropriations. To meet financial shortcomings, the army was reduced in size. MacArthur strove to preserve the officer corps.

In the summer of 1932, a horde of military veterans marched on Washington, D.C., and camped on the steps of the Capitol. They wanted a bonus due them for past services. Political leaders became frightened. They feared the government might be taken over by mob rule. General MacArthur, as head of the army, was called upon to clear the marchers out of the city. Although he found the task "as bitter as gall," he did as instructed. His opinions in the matter became controversial. Claiming that the bonus marchers were both Communists and Communist controlled, he labeled them nothing but radicals and criminals. He made several public statements to this effect. The name MacArthur sank low. Church leaders, veterans' organizations, the Congress, and the public press railed against him.

During 1935–36, Douglas MacArthur took a drastic step. He resigned his position as chief of staff and retired from the U.S. Army. He then moved to the Philippines, where he became that country's top military leader with the rank of field marshal. This appeared to be a foolhardy move, for the Philippine government was almost entirely without any army. He proposed universal military training to make up a large citizen army. To augment such a force, he planned a sizeable fleet of what he liked to call "Q boats." In reality they were PT (patrol torpedo) boats. Since the Philippines consist of more than 7,000 islands, with a combined

coastline greater than that of the United States, American admirals scoffed at such a plan. MacArthur, despite such strong opposition, insisted on having his fleet of torpedo boats.

During these days, relationships between the United States and Japan seemed headed for a clash. During July of 1941, Douglas MacArthur was recalled to active duty by the U.S. Army. He was then appointed commanding general, United States forces in the Far East. On December 7, 1941, at Pearl Harbor, Hawaii, the Japanese expressed their true military ambitions by attacking that city. A few days later they struck at three points in northernmost Luzon, in the Philippines. On December 22, an additional 45,000 Japanese landed at Lingayen Gulf, north of Manila. On December 24, strong elements of the Japanese army came ashore at Lamon Bay, south of Manila. American-Philippine supplies were running low. They had little with which to defend themselves. MacArthur, in accordance with prewar plans, withdrew his headquarters to Corregidor, a heavily fortified island at the entrance of Manila Bay. President Roosevelt ordered MacArthur to leave Corregidor and take up headquarters in Australia. It was then, on leaving, he uttered these famous words, "I shall return." Even for this statement he was criticized, as most people seem to feel that the word *we* should have been used in place of *I*. Nevertheless, for his defense of the Philippines, MacArthur received the Congressional Medal of Honor.

In 1942, MacArthur was named supreme commander of all Allied Forces, in the Southwest Pacific. This consisted of the Philippines, the Indies, Australia, and the United States. At once, he

MacArthur, with his second-in-command, Colonel Dwight D. Eisenhower, led troops against the bonus marchers in Washington, D.C.

[41]

began to protest America's agreement with the British to conquer Hitler before lending all-out assistance to the Pacific. Ironically, the American public knew little or nothing about land masses in the Pacific. Such faraway spots as Midway and Wake were places seldom mentioned even in a classroom. Suddenly, they became important to everyone. They became words that stood for suffering, death, and capture by the Japanese. Untold numbers of Americans were involved. Action was fast, with no one knowing for sure who was winning the Pacific War. The Japanese thrust their best ground troops and ships into the fray. We won some battles; they won some battles. The cost on both sides was heavy. Finally, American forces put up fierce resistance on New Guinea. Japan threw a vast military force against the Allies. Fighting was intense. America held. By bold use of air and sea power, MacArthur was beginning to show definite results with limited resources. The U.S. Pacific Fleet, under Admiral Chester Nimitz, won victories at the Coral Sea and Midway. Marines landed on Guadalcanal, and by September of 1942, the Japanese thrust to reach Australia was stalled. Slowly, Allied forces under MacArthur began to regain lost ground. In October of 1944, Leyte in the Philippines was invaded.

Leyte proved to be a horrendous defeat for the Japanese defenders. They lost more than 65,000 troops, a great portion of their fleet, millions of dollars worth of military equipment, and almost all their fighter planes—except for kamikazes.

The Japanese word *kamikaze* means "divine wind." It stood for suicide planes that dove for the flight decks of American aircraft carriers. It was at Leyte that Americans first experienced strikes by these suicidal planes. In 1945, kamikaze flights took a horrible toll of American ships. Their use was so successful, Japanese military forces launched thousands of such airplanes from an area called Kyushu. Although they took a heavy toll, they proved to be only a deterrent. Kamikaze flights in themselves could not win a war.

January 9, 1945 saw four divisions of Allied forces at Lingayen Gulf. Again, as at Leyte, MacArthur waded ashore to the island of

Luzon. It was not a pushover. Fighting was intense. MacArthur, however, took personal command, as well as many personal risks. Allied troops slowly closed in on Manila. On February 4, advance forces of the First Cavalry Division reached the outskirts of the city. MacArthur announced the fall of the city three days later.

By now General MacArthur had received his fifth star and had been promoted to General of the Army. Almost simultaneously with this event and the successful Philippine landings, the Japanese high command began to issue exaggerated claims about their victories. Field Marshal Count Hisaichi Terauchi, commander of Nippon forces in the Southwest Pacific, was beginning to believe propaganda put out by his own headquarters. Field-grade Japanese officers fighting in the islands soon learned what was expected of them. They reported shooting down clouds of Allied planes and sinking fleets of enemy ships. At one point, a badly shot-up squadron of Zeros returned to base and reported they had sunk numerous United States cruisers, several battleships, a number of aircraft carriers, and a destroyer or two. So great was the reported victory, a national holiday was proclaimed in Tokyo. The truth came as a bitter pill. The facts were, on the day of this supposed victory, the Japanese had lost 400 planes, while sinking but one American warship.

This was the beginning of the end for the Japanese. What were left of ground forces were poorly trained and badly equipped. Ammunition and rations were low and, in some instances, had reached a point of exhaustion. Regardless of what they were told, Allied planes continued to beat at them night and day. It was as if their own Zeros never existed. Yet Nippon radio reports were full of glowing victories. Japanese soldiers were brave enough, and willing to die for the Emperor, but could hardly be expected to fight with only their bare hands. Morale turned bad; the spirit of resistance crumbled. On August 6, an atomic bomb, with a force equal to 20,000 tons of TNT was dropped on Hiroshima. On August 9, another such bomb was dropped on Nagasaki. On August 15, Emperor Hirohito ordered his forces to cease fighting

[43]

and lay down their arms. Over the radio he told his subjects they must be prepared to suffer the insufferable. On September 2, 1945, aboard the American battleship *Missouri*, anchored in Tokyo Bay, the Japanese signed an agreement of surrender with General Douglas MacArthur.

President Franklin Roosevelt had died in the early part of 1945, and President Harry S Truman was in the White House. After having suspended all fighting, and with the approval of British Prime Minister Clement Attlee, Soviet ruler Joseph Stalin, and China's President Chiang Kai-shek, he named MacArthur supreme commander in Japan for the Allied powers (SCAP).

It was then that MacArthur, the victorious warrior, embarked on a peacetime command that was to earn him the respect and gratitude of the Japanese people as he oversaw the reconstruction of a shattered nation. In a series of decisive actions, he disarmed the Japanese military, instituted land reforms, and supervised the writing of a new, more democratic constitution.

It is probable that he would have ended his military career amid praise and panoply for these remarkable achievements had it not been for Korea.

In the closing days of World War II, it was agreed among the Allies that Russia would accept the surrender of Japanese troops in the northern part of Korea and the United States would accept the surrender of troops in the southern part. To this end, the thirty-eighth parallel, effectively dividing the country in half, was agreed upon as the border between the two nations' areas of responsibility—and, as it turned out, influence.

In the north, there was industry; in the south, agriculture. Rul-

*MacArthur, as Supreme Allied
Commander, accepts the
surrender of the Japanese
aboard the battleship* Missouri.

[45]

ing the northern half was a former guerrilla leader named Kim Il Sung. Under Communist domination, he set up what was called the Democratic People's Republic. In the south, Syngman Rhee was elected president of the Republic of Korea. He, of course, was backed by the United States. The North Koreans established their capital in Pyongyang; the South in a city called Seoul.

Here then was a divided country that most Americans knew little about and, to be truthful, weren't concerned over—until Sunday June 25, 1950, when war broke out. As cannon fire erupted from the north, with it came a swarm of well-armed North Korean soldiers, together with their Russian military advisers. The United Nations acted quickly. A resolution was passed, condemning North Korea's action, and subsequently, troops from fifteen member nations were sent to repel the invasion. Ill-prepared and outnumbered, the United Nations forces retreated south—all the way to the tip of Korea. There they rallied, then fought back. MacArthur, directing the counterattack, made a landing at Inchon, on the west coast behind North Korean lines, and caught the Communists off balance. They fell back to within their own territory and were scattered. Against orders that were perplexing and somewhat muddled, and contrary to United States policy, MacArthur used American troops to push on north to the Yalu River. This, it is believed by many, is what brought the Chinese Communists into the war. President Truman publicly stated that, "General MacArthur had openly defied the policy of his Commander in Chief, the President of the United States."

The Korean War continued until 1953 when a truce was signed, but in April of 1951, President Truman, angered at MacArthur's choosing to interpret orders to suit his own needs, relieved MacArthur of his command and recalled him to the United States.

Upon his arrival he received a hero's welcome. Invited to address a joint session of Congress, he gave a moving speech that was broadcast nationwide. In conclusion he said, "Old soldiers never die, they just fade away."

In 1952, there was an attempt to nominate him for the presidency. This failed. He then became an executive with a large industrial corporation. In Walter Reed Army Hospital, on April 5, 1964, MacArthur died. He was buried at Norfolk, Virginia.

Place of birth: Gladwyne, a suburb of Philadelphia, Pennsylvania.

Date of birth: June 25, 1886.

Date of death: January 15, 1950.

Education: West Point, class of 1907.

Married: Eleanor A. Pool, September 10, 1913.

Characteristics: Hot-tempered, calm under stress, enjoyed sports and poker, thoughtful, at times dogmatic, persistent, diplomatic, capable, reliable, sense of honor.

Major commands and accomplishments:
1907 Twenty-ninth Infantry Division, Philippines.
1911 Signal Corps, Dayton, Ohio, for flight training.
1912 Signal Corps Aviation School, College Park, Maryland.
1913 Thirteenth Infantry Division, Philippines.
1916 Aviation School, Rockwell Field, San Diego.
1917 Panama.
1918 European assignment.
1938 named chief of the Army Air Corps.
1942 named chief of the Army Air Forces.
1943 promoted to full general.
1944 promoted to five-star rank, general of the Air Force.

HENRY H. (HAP) ARNOLD

June 25, 1886 was an important day in the life of Dr. and Mrs. H. A. Arnold. A second son had been born to this family living in the suburbs of Philadelphia, Pennsylvania. The newborn child was named Henry Harley Arnold.

Ironically, the medically minded father planned for Henry to be a minister of the gospel, and for this purpose he was scheduled to attend Bucknell College. It was his older brother Tom who was slated to become a West Point graduate. However, as often happens, youngsters have a way of deciding their own future. Tom rejected the life of a soldier, deciding on engineering at Pennsylvania State University instead. Henry took the examinations for entry into West Point. He did well and in 1903 started his Plebe (freshman) year. This was the same year two bicycle repairmen named Wilbur and Orville Wright made their heroic twelve-second airplane flight near Kitty Hawk, North Carolina.

By his own admission, Henry Harley Arnold had happy years at West Point. As a result, his classmates dubbed him "Hap," a nickname that was to cling to him throughout the remainder of his life. And happy he must have been, for his record at the Point indicates that he was a prankster. As a result, he was disciplined for numerous minor breaches of regulations. In fact, when his future wife paid her first visit to West Point, it was to find that the man she loved had been placed in military confinement within his room.

During Arnold's four years at the Point, mounted troops trained to fight from horseback were the glamour boys of the military. The development of new and more deadly weapons, such as the machine gun and bolt-action rifle, brought trench warfare into vogue. This practically eliminated the combat use of cavalry. Regardless, traditions die hard. During these years prior to World War I, the cavalryman was still considered the elite of fighting forces. Like most of the West Point class, Hap wanted to be assigned to this branch of the service. He put in a request for cavalry duty. Promptly, upon graduation in 1907, he was issued orders dispatching him to the Twenty-ninth Infantry Division in the Philippines as a second lieutenant. He was furious and contemplated resigning from the service. However, he was talked out of such action and went on to report to his duty station.

Fate has a peculiar way of molding young lives. It was no different with Second Lieutenant Arnold. In 1909, returning to the United States by way of Europe, he found himself in Paris. As he walked the streets, he unexpectedly came upon a peculiar contraption on public display. It was an airplane—the first he had ever seen. This one, however, was not just any airplane. It was the machine in which a Frenchman named Louis Bleriot, on the twenty-fifth of July, 1909, had flown across the English Channel. This was considered a daring achievement, and the French were justly proud of such a long flight. The sight of the aircraft both interested and excited Hap Arnold. It was then he resolved to be a flyer.

On reporting for duty at Governors Island, New York, Second Lieutenant Arnold had the pleasure of meeting the great inventor Wilbur Wright. This was followed by a plane being landed on the island by Glenn Curtiss, already a well-known person in the fly-

[50]

ing business. As a follow up to these chance meetings, Hap Arnold attended the first American international air meet, held at Belmont Park, New York. There, most of the famed personalities in what was called "the flying game" assembled to show their aircraft and give performances. It was breathtakingly exciting. Hap Arnold wasted no time in taking advantage of the fact the U.S. Army was now experimenting with aircraft. Because of the high rate of mortality, they were looking for volunteers. Hap Arnold was both willing and able to take whatever chances were necessary.

On April 21, 1911, Second Lieutenant Arnold was ordered to report to the Signal Corps at Dayton, Ohio. On doing so, he was directed to a farm called Simms Station. It was a cow pasture, later to become known as Huffman Field. As Hap himself described the place, it was just another unplowed field loaned without charge by a patriotic farmer. One feature set it apart from all other fields. Each day, a local mortician would park his wagon, loaded with several wooden caskets, on the fringe of the field, there to sit and wait for business to drop in on him. All too often, a Wright Brothers student complied. Flying was risky business.

The Wright planes used by the government at that time were an improvement of the one flown at Kitty Hawk. They were capable of carrying two men in continuous flight for one hour, at a speed of not less than 40 miles (64 km) per hour. The first of these planes cost the army $25,000. The price included the training of two pilots for each plane purchased. It was at this time that a Lieutenant Benjamin D. Foulois was sent to Fort Sam Houston, Texas, together with a previously wrecked aircraft, and told to repair the plane and then teach himself to fly. He did just that. Such was the state of the art.

Hap Arnold, while in the Wright Brothers' factory, learned to fly in a rear room where an old plane was supported on two saw horses. During this incubation period, he made the acquaintance of many already famous pilots. One was Orville Wright's first student, a nineteen-year-old boy, who became popular for his

Above: *an airplane of the type first flown by Hap Arnold.* Facing: *Arnold in a Wright Type B airplane, May 1912*

mature saying to the effect that, "I would rather be the oldest living pilot in America than the best."

It was also during these days that a pilot named C. P. Rodgers made the first continental flight from New York to Los Angeles. The trip required forty-nine days, and was successful only because a railroad train followed along with a machine shop. The plane had to be repaired after each landing.

A pilot known as Al Walsh was assigned to be Arnold's instructor. On May 3, 1911, the two took their first training flight. It lasted seven minutes. Under a column headed "Remarks" on his flight-evaluation sheet, the instructor wrote the single word "Rough." It was never explained if this applied to the aircraft, the weather, or the student. At the end of the training flight that was numbered twenty-eighth, during which Arnold had spent a total of three hours and forty-eight minutes in the air, he was graduated, to become U.S. military aviator number four.

Hap Arnold was then sent by train, along with his aircraft, to College Park, Maryland. College Park was to be the Signal Corps Aviation School. It consisted of four hangars adjacent to the railroad tracks, a small administration shack, and an emergency hospital tent. As Arnold later remarked, "Our first job was to teach our immediate superiors how to fly." This made for a peculiar school, wherein the pupils knew more than their teachers. However, with everyone working in harmony, the school soon developed a set of standards that had to be met before a student could be called "military aviator." In part, these requirements were

that the student be able to fly his aircraft to an altitude of 2,500 feet (762 m); then be able to fly his machine in a wind of fifteen miles (24 km) per hour, and carry a passenger to 500 feet (152 m); that he make a dead-stick landing within 150 feet (45.7 m) of a given marker; that he be able to make a military reconnaissance flight of 20 miles (32 km) cross-country at an average altitude of 1,500 feet (457 m).

For Hap Arnold, these were days of trial and error. Experiments were interspersed with crashes, some successes, and too many fatalities. It was in 1912 that a young and inquisitive army captain arrived at College Park. Although not an aviator himself, the captain appeared to be aware of the advantages inherent in aviation. His name was Billy Mitchell, a man who was later to be court-martialed for his aggressive and progressive ideas about the use of army aviation.

It was not until the summer of 1912 that the U.S. Army took delivery of its first tractor plane, which meant that the engine was in front of the pilot, instead of to the rear. Hap Arnold was the pilot designated to accept delivery of the aircraft. It was fitted with a seventy-horsepower Renault engine. Unfortunately, it was a float plane and needed water to both take off and land. On the second day of the delivery flight, the plane was overloaded and, in turning away from the village of South Duxbury, Massachusetts, side-slipped and crashed into the water. A float was smashed, a wing crumpled, and Arnold slightly injured. The Coast Guard sent out a cutter that towed the aircraft into harbor. The plane was later repaired and shipped by rail to College Park.

In October of 1912, Hap Arnold received the much coveted Mackay Trophy. This was presented to him for the greatest contribution to aviation for the year of 1912. It was awarded for outstanding work in connection with army ground maneuvers. It was also during this year that the new "Military Aviator's Badge, " was given him. Both he and the army now officially had wings. Unfortunately, morale among aviators was low. Too many fatal accidents were occurring. To correct this situation, "flight pay" was authorized. This was a bonus of 35 percent of base pay. It helped to some degree, but many pilots were growing nervous because of aviation's overall accident rate.

In September of 1913, Hap Arnold and Eleanor A. Pool were married. During December of 1913, he was assigned to duty with the Thirteenth Infantry in the Philippines. In 1915, Hap and Eleanor had their first of four children; a girl, Lois, was born in Manila.

Things were happening in Europe. World War I was under way. In May of 1916, Lieutenant Hap Arnold was assigned to the newly formed Aviation School at Rockwell Field, San Diego, as supply officer. The school consisted of twenty-three military aviators, twenty-five students, and an uncertain number of tractor-type planes. The mountains and deserts of the West were the setting for the development of search-and-rescue techniques for downed pilots. It was at this task that Hap Arnold worked. As a culmination, he was given command of the Seventh Aero Squadron, in Panama. This was an organization he was supposed to establish as part of military protection afforded the canal. At that time it was nonexistent.

Ordered back to Washington, D.C., Arnold was aboard a ship headed for New York harbor when word was received by wireless that the United States had declared war on Germany. That altered his career. He was transferred to Carlstrom Field, Florida, as commander of a pursuit school. His job was to turn army men into fighter pilots.

The first American aviators to fly against German pilots during World War I had been formed into the French Lafayette Escadrille and were already establishing an impressive record. They were the envy of every U.S. Army military aviator, including Hap Arnold. He requested duty in Europe. In this he had no luck. However, in other things he was more fortunate. By August of 1917, he had been promoted to full colonel, the youngest one in the army. This made him the senior officer in Washington with wings.

Hap Arnold still wanted a European assignment. Finally, after much persistence, he was ordered to a combat unit overseas. With great expectations, he hurriedly left the States, to arrive in Europe on November 11, 1918—the day peace was declared. Within less than a year, and without seeing combat, he was returned to the United States. The Army Air Service had proven itself and in 1919

*Arnold is shown here on the left
in a tractor-type airplane in 1916.*

consisted of hundreds of planes, 16,500 enlisted men, and 1,500 flying officers in one stage or another of development. Accidents, through carelessness and poor judgment, were numerous. It was at this time the U.S. Army Air Service issued its Flying Regulations consisting of twenty-seven points. These, although important at the time, sound a bit absurd in this day and age of jet aircraft. For instance, to name but a few: aviators will not wear spurs while flying; if engine stops, land as soon as you can; pilots should carry handkerchiefs in a handy position to wipe off goggles; don't take the machine into the air unless you are satisfied it will fly.

Aviation politics now exploded within the American military establishment. General William Mitchell, assistant chief of the Air Service, clashed with the army and navy top echelons. In the end, despite his fine war record, Billy Mitchell resigned from the service. On February 19, 1936, Mitchell died at the age of fifty-six. During World War II his prophecies proved themselves accurate and he was posthumously awarded a special Medal of Honor. Billy Mitchell and Charles Lindbergh were the first two aviators ever to receive this nation's highest award in peacetime.

As the years dragged on, Hap Arnold worked at keeping the Army Air Service in the public eye. He created the U.S. Air Mail, flew patrol missions for the Forestry Service, and continually pushed both his men and his flying machines to their maximum. He also became an advocate for an independent air force. His name was linked with the development of large, four-engined bombers. This was a new and experimental concept in aviation.

During 1938, Arnold was promoted to major general and named chief of the Army Air Corps. It was at this time the world became aware of the rise of totalitarian regimes in Germany, Italy, and Japan. This upsurge was attributed to the great depression that gripped the world in the early 1930s, and from unsatisfactory peace terms that followed World War I. As a consequence, in 1939, when Germany invaded Poland and Italy invaded Albania, both England and France were forced to declare war on Hitler and Mussolini. World War II was under way.

Through General Arnold's forceful leadership, the wartime air service began its growth from fewer than 25,000 officers and men, plus 4,000 planes, to 2.5 million officers and men, with 75,000 aircraft. Hap Arnold's rank and title advanced accordingly. In June of 1941, he was named chief of the United States Army Air Forces and in December was promoted to lieutenant general. In this position of power, Hap Arnold pushed a multi-million-dollar gamble. He wanted the world's most powerful four-engined bomber, with long-range capabilities. Out of his insistence came the Boeing Superfortress B-29 bomber. Here was an aircraft that could carry up to ten tons of bombs, mount eight .50-caliber machine guns in remote-controlled turrets and a twenty-millimeter cannon in a tail turret. Four Wright twin-tow radial engines, each of 2,200 horsepower, drove the B-29 to an all-out speed of 365 miles per hour (587 km) at an altitude of 25,000 feet (7,620 m). With a cruising speed of 220 miles per hour (354 km), the B-29 possessed a maximum span of 5,830 miles (9,380 km).

The design, development, and production of the aircraft was a wild throw of the dice by Hap Arnold. Through his efforts, the army ordered almost 300 of these aircraft even before Boeing had a chance to complete a mock-up. There were those in the military who thought the gamble foolhardy and fought to prevent the plane's development. Regardless, Arnold had confidence in what he had learned long ago about aircraft—given enough power and good men to handle them, they could complete outstanding missions. The B-29, with a dead weight of over 100,000 pounds (50,000 kg), a wingspread of 141 feet (43 m), and length of 99 feet (30 m), made its first strike on June 5, 1944. Nine days later, the B-29 bomber hit its first target in Japan.

During March of 1943, Hap Arnold received a fourth star and late in 1944 received his fifth. Hap Arnold's development and applied tactics of the B-29 had taken less than four years. In all,

this dream in the mind of one man flew 35,000 missions and dropped about 175,000 tons (158,725 mt) of bombs on the enemy. In the end, it was the plane that loosed an atomic bomb over Hiroshima and another on Nagasaki.

President Truman appointed Hap Arnold to the five-star rank of General of the Air Force. This was on June 3, 1949, and, although Arnold was already a five-star general of the Army, this Air Force commission was the first ever awarded. It was bestowed on him for his many air-related achievements, trophies, and foreign awards. In all, Hap Arnold had twice won the Mackay Trophy, as well as the Collier Trophy, two Distinguished Service Medals, the Air Medal, and the Distinguished Flying Cross. In addition, his foreign awards and commendations were almost too numerous to count.

Hap Arnold died at sixty-three years of age, on January 15, 1950. He is buried at the National Cemetery in Washington, D.C.

General of the Army
Hap Arnold

Place of birth: San Gabriel, California.

Date of birth: November 11, 1885.

Date of death: December 21, 1945.

Education: West Point, class of 1909.

Married: Beatrice Banning Ayer, on May 26, 1910.

Characteristics: Self-confident, enthusiastic, loyal, self-disciplined, showman, love of reading the classics.

Major commands and assignments:
1916 accompanied General Pershing to Mexico.
1917 commanded 304th Brigade Tank Corps in France.
1940 brigade commander Second Armored Division.
1942 commander of Western Task Force, Operation Torch, Northwest Africa.
1943 assisted in organizing Seventh Army for invasion of Sicily.
1943 commanded Second Corps.
1944 commanded Third Army.
1945 named military governor of Bavaria.

GEORGE S. PATTON, JR.

The enemy came sweeping around the barn, guns blazing, sabres slashing the air. This was their third bloody attempt to capture the ranch house. Each charge had been defeated by a six-year-old boy armed with a wooden sword, a uniform hat made from a folded newspaper, and a handgun carved out of the branch of a tree.

Abruptly, there was a lull in the battle. Aunt Annie's strident voice hit the battlefield. "George Patton, Jr., put down those toys and come into this house at once—your lunch is ready."

The warrior acted as though he had not heard. The battle continued. Soldiers, the boy reasoned—the real fighting kind—never stopped battling simply because of an empty stomach. They fought and fought until the enemy was vanquished.

Again that voice. This time it bugled a more enticing call. "George Patton, Jr., there'll be no reading session this afternoon unless you come eat your lunch, *immediately!*"

The boy dropped his sword, tossed aside his wooden gun and came racing. After all, Aunt Annie, the unmarried aunt of the Patton family, was well into the second half of *King Arthur and the Knights of the Round Table*—his favorite story.

In fact, as the boy grew into manhood and later into a caval-

ryman, his favorite horse would always be named Galahad, and his pet dog Lancelot—both names belonging to fearless knights of King Arthur's round table.

But there were many troublesome years of growing up yet to be overcome before George S. Patton, Jr., would have a war-horse of his own to name Galahad. Pat, as he was later called by school chums, had a strong family military tradition to equal. Hugh Mercer, a brigadier general (one star), in the Continental Army, was George Patton's great-grandfather. He died from bayonet wounds and a British musket ball at the battle of Trenton, on December 26, 1776. His grandfather, a colonel in the Confederate army was killed during the Civil War, at the Second Battle of Winchester. His father, George S. Patton, Sr., was a graduate of V.M.I. (Virginia Military Institute). At twelve, George Jr., went to Stephen Cutter Clark's Classical School for Boys, in Pasadena, California, for his first bit of formal schooling. Following that, he attended and graduated from Pasadena High School. During these years, education was a grind to the young student. He proved himself poor at mathematics, and a miserable speller, with no sense of punctuation.

Throughout his boyhood and early education, Pat had one outspoken ambition—to be a soldier. To attain this end, he applied for admission to West Point. At that time, California had no allotted appointments to the academy. Not to be deterred, he entered V.M.I., the renowned military academy from which his father had graduated. He completed one year as a "rat" (freshman), at the end of which he was admitted to West Point. He arrived there in June 1904 as a candidate, or yearling cadet.

Haunted by an indifference toward mathematics, he put emphasis on military subjects, sports, and self-discipline. Regard-

George Patton, Jr.,
at age seven

less of his poor academic showing and having to repeat his fourth year, Pat was named adjutant and first captain of the entire corps, a great honor. It was during June week of his fifth year as a cadet at West Point, that soon-to-be Second Lieutenant Patton proposed to a young woman named Beatrice Banning Ayer. She was the daughter of a multi-millionaire from Boston, Massachusetts. The two had been secretly in love for many years. However, almost another twelve months were to slide by before Pat and Bea took their vows of marriage in the Beverly Farms Episcopal Church, Pride's Crossing, Massachusetts.

The cavalry was known as the rip-roaring branch of the U.S. Army. For that reason, Pat, while still a student at the Point, had honed his studies and physique toward becoming a cavalryman. On graduation, his first assignment as a second lieutenant was to Troop K, Fifteenth Cavalry, based at Fort Sheridan, Illinois. It was to that post he took his bride, where the two lived in a tiny unit in a row of duplex houses. Gone were the gold and tinsel days as a West Point cadet. Here was the hard core grind of military life. The young couple stood at the bottom of a long and arduous ladder yet to be climbed.

George, to relieve the energies that flamed within his soul, took to mastering the art of polo. Bea, his adoring wife, being proficient in French, stimulated his military mind by translating French cavalry regulations for his own application. French cavalrymen, at that time, were thought to be the greatest equestrians in the world.

Then came the big event. On March 11, 1911, a daughter was born to the Patton couple. She was named Beatrice in honor of her mother. In December of that same year came the couple's first transfer. Lieutenant George S. Patton, Jr., was directed to report to the commandant, Fort Myer, Virginia. There he continued his studies in cavalry tactics and worked at becoming a number one polo player. It was not long before the young officer came to the attention of his superiors as both an athlete and a cavalryman.

As a consequence of his constant hard riding and physical

conditioning, Lieutenant Patton was a natural selection for the 1912 International Pentathlon. This was to be held in Sweden and consisted of five soldierly accomplishments: first, pistol marksmanship; second, swordsmanship; third, personal combat; fourth, horsemanship; and, fifth, a grueling foot race. There was no time allotted between events. Once under way, it was finish—or drop dead trying, which one contestant did. George Patton staggered across the finish line, number five amidst a field of over forty of the world's finest athletes. A proud accomplishment for any young man.

In all likelihood, because of this fine showing, George Patton was ordered to France to study that country's advanced theories in the use of mounted troops. Shortly thereafter, he received another permanent change of station. His destination was the Mounted Service School, Fort Riley, Kansas. There he was assigned as an instructor in the use of the saber. During this period he wrote the U.S. *Manual on Saber Regulations*. This manual remained standard until midway through World War I. At that time, both the cavalry and the saber were discontinued in favor of trench warfare.

During this period, Mexico was in the throes of a revolution that would eventually lead to improved living conditions for the farmers and the establishment of a democratic government. In 1916, a Mexican revolutionary general named Pancho Villa, was causing trouble along the Mexican border. George Patton, now with the Eighth Cavalry, was on patrol in a desolate area called Sierra Blanca. Suddenly Villa overplayed his hand. With a force close to 500, he crossed the border into New Mexico. There he completely destroyed the town of Columbus. In doing so, he killed a small detachment of soldiers from the Thirteenth Cavalry, as well as a number of civilians. He then returned across the border into Mexico.

General John J. (Black Jack) Pershing, then positioned with a force at El Paso, Texas, was ordered by President Woodrow Wilson to pursue Villa into Mexico. General Pershing formed a quick-strike force that, unfortunately for Patton, did not include the Eighth Cavalry. Wanting to accompany the general, and not to be thwarted, Patton went to Pershing's outer office, where he settled himself into a chair and waited. Finally, after forty hours had passed, Pershing began to wonder who the second lieutenant was seated in his outer office. Out of curiosity he asked, "Who are you and what do you want?"

"Lieutenant Patton, sir. I've been wanting a chance to talk with you."

"What is it you want?"

"To go with you to Mexico, as one of your aides, sir."

"I've already selected my two aides."

"Sir, you could very likely use a third aide, and if you take me, sir, I can promise you'll never regret it."

Pershing shrugged him off, but did mention that Patton might hear from him later. In fact, he was so interested in the young man, he did take him along as a "special aide." And as it turned out, the general never did regret it. For at one point in their pursuit of Villa, Pershing dispatched several patrols to search a sector called Lake Itaskate. It was rumored that one of the Mexican generals, a man named Lazaro Cardenas, was in that area. Patton was in charge of one patrol from Troop C, Thirteenth Cavalry. Wearing his white-handled .45 caliber Peacemaker revolver, Patton, through a series of unforeseen events, managed to come upon the Mexican general in a ranch house. A shoot-out followed.

Later, Patton drove up to Pershing's headquarters in an automobile. Across each front fender lay the body of a man.

While serving as an aide to General Pershing in Mexico in 1916, Patton participated in his first combat.

"Who are they?" Pershing asked.

"General Cardenas and an assistant named Lopez, sir."

General Pershing was so impressed that he promoted Patton to first lieutenant on the spot. That night, in the secrecy of his own tent, Patton cut two notches in the grip of his Peacemaker revolver. That Colt handgun, registration number 332099, is on display in the West Point Museum.

During these years of border troubles with Mexico, a much more severe war had broken out in Europe. World War I was well under way, with the United States slowly being sucked into the vortex. Finally, on April 6, 1917, President Wilson declared war on Germany. His aim, so he proclaimed, was "to make the world safe for democracy."

General Pershing was ordered to form the American Expeditionary Force. On May 26, 1917, he officially took command of what was little more than a paper military force. America, over the years, had neglected its military might and let it wither into almost nothingness. This was Patton's chance to forge ahead. He boarded a troop ship scheduled to sail on May 29 of that year. There were two noticeable differences about this zealous young officer. First, he wore the insignia of a captain. Second, in place of his white-handled Peacemaker revolver, he now carried an ivory-handled .45 caliber Colt automatic. It had his initials skillfully carved into its grip.

On November 19, 1917, while in Europe, Patton received special orders to report to the Commandant of Army Schools at Langres, France, for training in the use of tanks. His newly assigned job was to establish a tank corps for the American First Army. Hence, George S. Patton, Jr., became this nation's first tank soldier. The fact that at the time of his appointment he was without a single tank did not bother him. He begged and borrowed from the English and French, to the extent that he was given command of the 304th Tank Brigade. Now a temporary lieutenant colonel, he possessed 22 French Renault tanks, with 1,200 on order from the United States—an order, incidentally, that was not filled until after the armistice was signed on November 11, 1918.

Despite the inefficiencies and mechanical shortcomings of the French tanks (they were slow, wasted fuel, were thinly armored, could only crawl at five miles per hour, and were unable to cross ditches), Patton used them as he would a troop of cavalry.

By the time World War I was over, Patton had earned a Purple Heart for wounds suffered from machine-gun fire and shrapnel, the Distinguished Service Medal, and the Distinguished Service Cross. He returned aboard the troop transport *Patria*, arriving in New York during March of 1919, and was assigned to the Tank Center then at Camp Meade (now Fort Meade), Maryland. It was there he first met a Lieutenant Colonel Dwight D. Eisenhower, West Point class of 1915, who had been in charge of stateside tank training. A lasting friendship formed between these two men that was to serve Patton well during World War II. Both could foresee a great future for the armored divisions.

Unfortunately, Congress could not. As a result, not only were tank divisions cut to a minimum, but the entire United States military structure was dismantled. With what little was left to him, George Patton continued working out new maneuvers for mobile units and being a good father to his family. By now he had two additional children. Besides Beatrice, there was Ruth Ellen, born in 1915, and George, born in 1923.

Peacetime military life was discouraging to a man of action. Patton was cut back to his permanent rank of captain; shortly thereafter, he was promoted to major, then transferred to the cavalry at Fort Myer, Virginia. During April of 1925, he received orders sending him to Hawaii. There he was made intelligence officer. As an astute observer, he readily foresaw danger in the ease with which Japanese fishermen could come and go in and around the Hawaiian Islands. He wrote warning reports that he suspected many of the fishermen were Japanese reserve officers taking pictures and soundings of harbor areas. His reports were ignored.

In 1928, orders returned Patton to the mainland. This time he was assigned to the office of Chief of Cavalry, Washington, D.C. There, routine peacetime duties kept him busy until he regained his old rank of colonel. With that rank he was given command of the Fifth Cavalry, Fort Clark, Texas. However, a short time later, he was transferred to Fort Myer, Virginia, where he assumed command of the Third Cavalry. Meantime, on September 1, 1939, German armored divisions swept into Poland, clearly indicating the effectiveness of a quick-strike force.

In less than two years, Patton was promoted to the rank of temporary brigadier general (one star) and given command of the Second Armored Division, Fort Benning, Georgia. Soon thereafter, Patton was promoted to temporary major general (two stars). He was then placed in charge of an entire armored division.

Dressing in uniforms of his own design and carrying a brace of either pearl-handled revolvers, automatics, or target pistols, Patton nevertheless gave the division leadership and a high degree of morale.

General Patton, in the training of his divisions, is accredited with being the first field commander to use light, slow-flying aircraft as observation instruments. The practice was soon adopted by other commanders. Patton's ever-forceful ways gained him another step forward and in a short time he was awarded command of America's first and only armored corps. In preparedness for Hitler's armored divisions, Patton's corps was moved to desert country extending over parts of Nevada, Arizona, and California. This was in 1942. In July of that same year, General George C. Marshall, then chief of staff, named Patton commander of operation "Torch." This was to be an invasion of North Africa. Patton readied his task force with speed and enthusiasm. Early in November he stood aboard the cruiser *Augusta* ready to be put ashore. To save port facilities at Casablanca—for later Allied military use—he had chosen to direct his main thrust against a place known as the Pedhala area. On the eighth of that month, at 3:00 A.M., a U.S. Navy task force began to unload infantrymen down cargo nets and into small landing craft. All went smoothly until the coming of daylight revealed what was happening. French forces that had once been defeated by the Germans, and previously formed into their own Vichy government, now controlled this section of North Africa. Against prior commitments not to do so, these French forces opened fire against the Americans. This became a naval battle in which Patton, a cavalryman with iron horses, could not be landed. It was well into late afternoon before he could step ashore and take command.

It was then that the Patton legend of invincibility began to blossom. Wearing a pair of pearl-handled handguns, he began a great show of leadership. He seemed to be everywhere, giving physical assistance, as well as demonstrating leadership, to his American forces. He was actively on his feet and in battle for eighteen hours straight.

Once the arduous strain of battle was over, Patton was faced with the delicate task of gaining support of French Vichy authorities. In this undertaking, as well as in all others that marked his life, Patton switched from warrior to diplomat with ease. He proved to be shrewd, understanding, and charming. Being a man of winning ways, he gained control through a delicate balance of force and diplomacy.

Unfortunately for American forces, Rommel's Afrika Corps was grinding Allied troops to pieces. Unseasoned American tankers were overwhelmed by the Twenty-first Panzer Division. It was a horrible and bloody defeat for the United States. Out of desperation, General Eisenhower promoted Patton to lieutenant general (three stars) and put him in charge of the Second Corps. With that he issued orders that Patton—stationed some 2,000 miles away from Rommel's tanks—was to get busy and clear out the valley overrun by Germans. For Patton, this was a situation of put up or shut up. Over the past months he'd been blustering about how he'd like a chance to rub Rommel's face into the sand. Now the two were about to meet.

Early in 1941, Hitler had placed Field Marshal Rommel (the

Desert Fox), in command of the Afrika Corps. This move was to sustain the Italians in Libya. Orders given him were to maintain a defensive front only. However, by nature a trained, aggressive soldier, Rommel found no trouble in pushing the weaker British force back into Egypt. From mid-1941 until late 1942, Rommel dominated the North African theatre of war.

As a consequence, Patton assumed command of a defeated and dejected corps. Having noticed that the American troops dressed and acted with a defeatest attitude, he issued an order. It not only angered every man in the corps, it got results. He demanded that military personnel immediately begin wearing helmets, leggings, and neckties at all times. In the heat of North Africa, this seemed like needless punishment. However, General Bradley saw through the strategy and later wrote, "Each time a soldier knotted a necktie, threaded his leggings, and buckled on his steel helmet, he was forceably reminded that Patton had come to command the Second Corps . . . and with that a tough new era had begun."

Nurses, mechanics, doctors, chaplains, and tank commanders—all were included in the dress code. There were no exceptions. Yet Patton added a personal touch to this awareness of leadership. He constantly appeared on the front lines wherever the fighting was toughest and the going slow. His tactics worked. Within less than thirty days, the Sbeitla Valley was cleared of enemy. Unfortunately, Patton's ambitions to confront Rommel on the field of battle were thwarted. The German leader became ill and was returned to Germany.

General Patton attends a demonstration of tank-mounted flamethrowers during World War II.

Hitler refused the hard-pressed Afrika Corps either supplies or reinforcements. On March 6, 1943, the decisive battle of Medenine was fought. Combat opened with the first light of dawn and continued throughout the day. By evening the Axis forces had been decimated. The German-Italian struggle to hold North Africa had cost them dearly. Axis forces had lost close to 1,000,000 soldiers; in supplies, close to 3,000,000 tons destroyed or sunk in the Mediterranean. As a follow-up, General Eisenhower decided to invade Sicily. In keeping with this, Patton was ordered to turn the Second Corps over to General Omar Bradley and return to Morocco. There he was to help plan operation "Husky."

After months of rehearsal, Husky was launched on July 10, 1943. This Sicilian campaign was to have a two-fold effect on the minds of the American people. It confirmed General Patton as a national war hero and almost banished him from the military because of national hate. The love-hate affair began when Patton thrust his troops ashore, decimated the famed Hermann Göring Mechanized Division and, by his own brave leadership, prevented a near collapse of Allied invading forces.

The hate part took shape later. Patton, while visiting a hospital, slapped an enlisted man with his gloves for malingering. When this story broke in the national press, the American public found it revolting. They called for General Patton's immediate removal.

However, Eisenhower weighed both the good and the bad. Knowing that he had no other combat leader as aggressive as Patton, he hid the man's presence in a cloak of inactivity. The public soon forgot. There was a war going on. Day-by-day casualties occupied the headlines. Eleven months after the slapping incident, General Patton was quietly given command of the Third Army in January of 1944. He rapidly became an integral member of the Eisenhower-Bradley-Patton combo that smashed its way across Nazi-occupied Europe.

General Patton showed his true values when he detached three of his hard-hitting divisions and pushed them through ice and snow to reach the besieged area around Bastogne. This was a crucial road center in Belgium that gained fame as the scene for the Battle of the Bulge. However, one of his greatest displays of human understanding took place near Weimar. There his troops came upon a Nazi concentration camp known as Buchenwald. The sight of rotting corpses and dehumanized people both sickened and angered him. He ordered his troops to round up the inhabitants of Weimar—some estimated 1300 men and women—and to march them slowly through the entire camp. Many became ill, and one man returned to his home and committed suicide. At the end of the war, Patton's Third Army was across the borders of Czechoslovakia and Austria.

With the coming of peace in Europe, General Patton, now a four-star general, became too hot to handle. He advocated and suggested that now was the time for Allied forces to smash Communism. He publicly stated that, "If it's necessary to fight the Russians, the sooner we do it the better."

Fight talk of this nature, at a time when most Americans wanted little more than to get our boys home from Europe—and settle the Pacific War—was disturbing. It caused General Eisenhower a great deal of consternation.

During October of 1945, General Patton was removed from command of the Third Army. Two months later he was fatally injured when a truck rammed his staff car. He was buried close to Hamm, Luxembourg. A simple cross, placed at the head of those who died in the Third Army, marks his grave. Proud, even in death, he remains as the leader who covered more ground, with greater speed, and captured more prisoners, than any other general in the history of America.

INDEX

ABOUT THE AUTHOR

James B. Sweeney, a retired lieutenant colonel of the U.S. Air Force, has a long history of military service. As a combat reporter in World War II, he was awarded a Bronze Star, four Battle Stars, and several commendation medals.

Colonel Sweeney has written many books for young people. He is the author of *A Combat Reporter's Report* and *True Spy Stories*, both published by Franklin Watts.